Look   Puzzle   Learn

THE
GREAT
UNDERSEA
SEARCH

Kate Needham

Illustrated by Ian Jackson

Designed by Andy Griffin

Series editor:
Felicity Brooks

Scientific consultants:
Dr Margaret Rostron,
Dr John Rostron

Diving consultant:
Reg Vallintine

With thanks to Dr John
Bevan, Rachael Swann and
Sophy Tahta

Cover design: Helen Wood

This snake lives in the mangrove swamps. Find out what else lives there on pages 24 and 25.

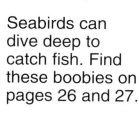

You can find penguins darting through the water off the Galapagos islands on pages 26 and 27.

Seabirds can dive deep to catch fish. Find these boobies on pages 26 and 27.

Learn about a diver's work under the sea on pages 22 and 23.

These underwater machines are used to repair oil rigs on pages 22 and 23.

Contents

Sea otters live in kelp forests. Find out who else lives in the kelp on pages 20 and 21.

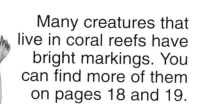

Many creatures that live in coral reefs have bright markings. You can find more of them on pages 18 and 19.

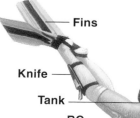

Fins

Knife

Tank

BC

Regulator

Find out about the equipment that divers use to breathe underwater on pages 18 and 19.

Discover which weird creatures live at the bottom of the sea on pages 16 and 17.

About this book

Ammonites lived over 200 million years ago. Find some other ancient creatures on pages 4 and 5.

In this book you can find out about all sorts of exciting things that happen under the sea, and discover the animals and plants that live there. There are puzzles to solve too. This shows you how they work.

Dangerous moray eels lurk in the shipwreck on pages 6 and 7.

There are hundreds of things to find in each big picture. In real life the seas are much less crowded.

Around the outside of each big picture are lots of little ones.

The blue writing next to each picture tells you how many of that thing you can find in the big picture.

Discover what you might find in pools among the rocks on pages 8 and 9.

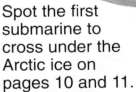

Spot the first submarine to cross under the Arctic ice on pages 10 and 11.

You can only see part of this shark but it still counts.

This manta ray in the distance counts.

You will need to count all these snakes carefully.

This shark coming out of the picture is here instead of the little picture. You do not count it in your total.

Find chests full of coins and more pirate treasure on pages 12 and 13.

The puzzle is to find all the things in the main picture. Some are easy, but others are tiny or partly hidden. Some animals look quite similar, so you will need to look very carefully to spot the difference. If you can't find something you can look up the answer on pages 28-31.

Turn to pages 16 and 17 to find out about the submersibles that explore the ocean depths.

Sailfish are the fastest fish in the sea. You'll find them on pages 14 and 15.

Turn to pages 14 and 15 to find the most dangerous shark of all.

Prehistoric seas

Ammonites used their tentacles to catch food. Find 13.

Banjo fish were ancient relatives of skates and rays. Can you see four more?

Ichthyosaurus gave birth under water. Find two adults and three babies.

Jellyfish lived up to 600 million years ago. Can you see four?

Giant sea turtles like archelon could hide inside their hard shells. Spot two.

Placodus had a very strong jaw. Find two.

Two hundred million years ago, dinosaurs ruled the land and giant creatures swam in the seas. Smaller ones lived there too. Some are still around today. Look closely to find 21 different creatures in this scene.

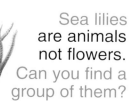

Sea lilies are animals not flowers. Can you find a group of them?

Rabbit fish get their name from their funny faces. Find two.

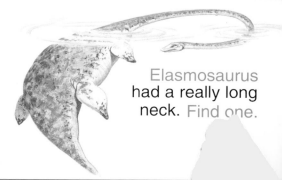

Elasmosaurus had a really long neck. Find one.

4

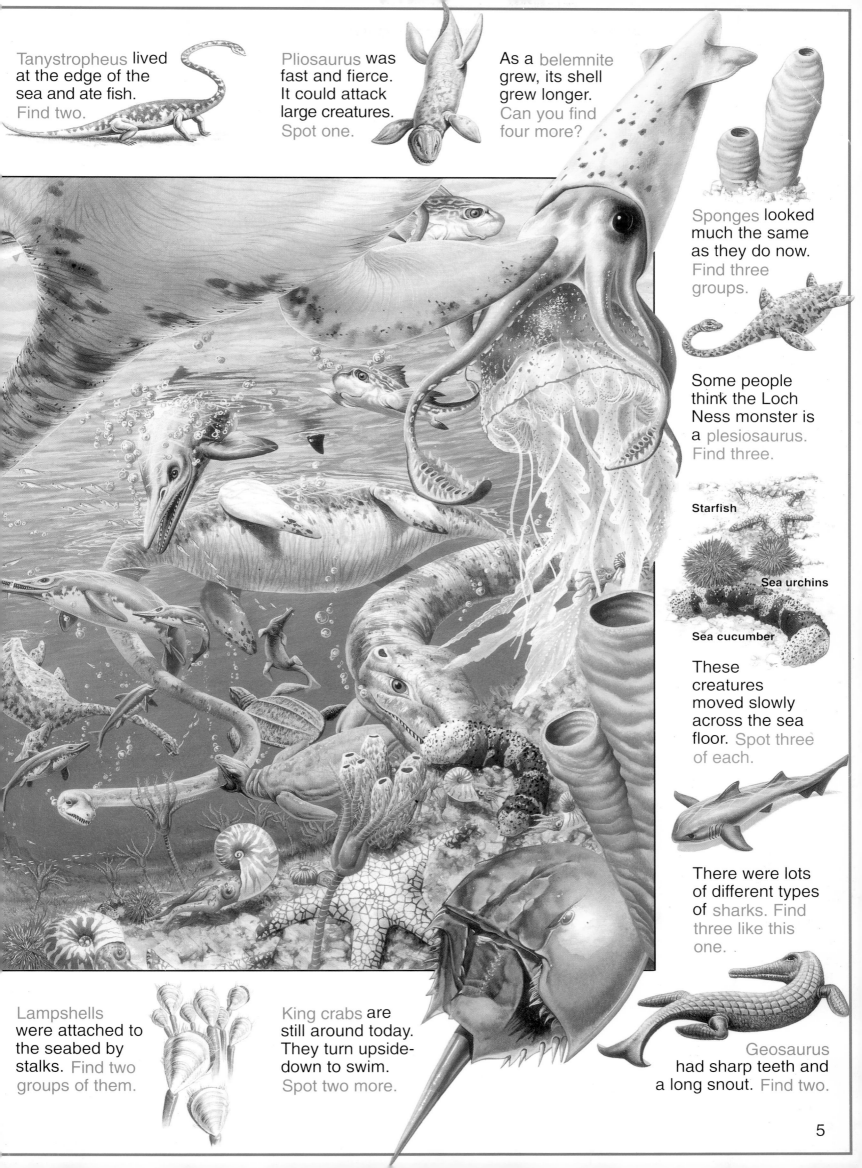

Tanystropheus lived at the edge of the sea and ate fish. Find two.

Pliosaurus was fast and fierce. It could attack large creatures. Spot one.

As a belemnite grew, its shell grew longer. Can you find four more?

Sponges looked much the same as they do now. Find three groups.

Some people think the Loch Ness monster is a plesiosaurus. Find three.

Starfish

Sea urchins

Sea cucumber

These creatures moved slowly across the sea floor. Spot three of each.

There were lots of different types of sharks. Find three like this one.

Lampshells were attached to the seabed by stalks. Find two groups of them.

King crabs are still around today. They turn upside-down to swim. Spot two more.

Geosaurus had sharp teeth and a long snout. Find two.

Shipwreck

All parts of a wreck are soon covered with coral. Can you find the anchor?

Reef sharks look dangerous but they rarely attack divers. Find three.

This ship was carrying bikes. Can you find three covered with coral?

Napoleon wrasses are large, friendly fish which often follow divers. Spot three.

With an eye and a nostril on each side of its wide head, a hammerhead shark sees and smells well. Find four more.

Some wrecks have hidden treasure. There are 18 gold bars to find here.

When you dive down to explore a wreck, you never know what you may find. There may be strange creatures lurking in the depths, or treasure buried in the sand. This ship sank years ago. Now it's covered in coral.

Crocodile fish have shiny green eyes. Spot one hiding on the sea bed.

Corals of all shades grow on the wreck. Spot four pink clumps.

Parrot fish nibble the corals with their beak-like mouths. Spot three.

This diver is going down to explore the wreck. Can you find seven more?

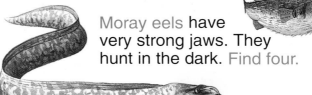

Moray eels have very strong jaws. They hunt in the dark. Find four.

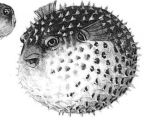

When they are scared, puffer fish blow up like spiky balloons. Can you see all four?

Spines

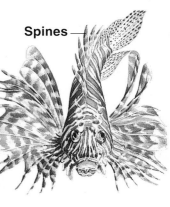

Lion fish have poisonous spines along their backs. Can you see two?

Cleaner fish clean the mouths and gills of larger fish. Spot four at work.

Blue spotted groupers like to live inside holes in the wreck. Find four.

These small fish recognize each other by their bright markings. Find 20 of each.

Angel fish

Butterfly fish

Anthias

Divers carry flashlights to see inside the darkest parts of a wreck. Spot four.

Glass fish swim around together in large groups called schools. Spot one school.

Common starfish

Cushion star

"Bloody Henry"

There are many types of starfish. Most have five arms. Spot four of each of these.

Beadlet anemones close up tightly to keep moist until the sea returns. Spot 20.

Hermit crabs live in empty shells. They move house as they grow. Can you find two?

Limpets

Mussels

Some animals that live in shells cling to the rocks. Find five groups of each of these.

Rocky shore

Kittiwakes live on the cliffs and fish in the sea. Can you count 50?

The sea comes in and out twice each day on this rocky shore. When it goes out, many creatures are left behind in pools among the rocks like this one. If you look closely you will find over 100 creatures here.

Grey seals have large eyes to see in cloudy water and thick fur to keep them warm. Spot nine.

Butterfish are long and thin with spots along their backs. Find four more.

With eyes on top of their heads, rock gobies can spot danger above. Find two.

8

Octopuses can squeeze into tiny spaces. Can you find one?

Some rocks have fossils like these ammonites in them. Find ten.

Oystercatchers use their sharp beaks to eat shellfish. Spot three more.

Shore crab

Edible crab

Velvet swimming crab

Crabs can give a painful nip if you pick them up. Find three of each type.

Blennies use their fins to walk to a new pool. Spot three.

Acorn barnacles attach themselves to any hard surface. Find some on rocks, crabs and mussels.

Prawns are hard to spot as they are almost transparent. Find seven.

Can you see a net and bucket that someone has left behind?

Squat lobsters have huge front legs that are bigger than their bodies. Spot two.

Icy seas

Research ships have especially strong bows to break through the ice. Spot one.

When polar bears swim, a layer of fat and thick fur keeps them warm in the icy water. Spot four.

The Arctic Ocean is so cold that two-thirds of it is covered in ice all year round. Despite the freezing water, plenty of creatures live here. Scientists also visit to study the ice and learn about the world's changing climate.

Beluga whales are called "sea canaries" because they sing to each other. Spot three.

Baby seals are called pups. They have fluffy white coats. Spot three.

Nautilus was the first submarine to cross the Arctic under the ice. Can you see it?

Walruses can use their tusks to lever themselves out of the water. Find 15.

Scientists attach transmitters to some animals to find out how they live. Spot one.

Bearded seals use their long curly whiskers to find shellfish. Find three.

Male narwhals have a long spiral tusk that is actually a huge front tooth. Find eight.

Arctic terns fly from the very north to the very south of the world each year. Spot four.

Humpback whales sometimes leap right out of the water. Spot three.

Harp seal

Ringed seal

Ribbon seal

You can spot different seals by their markings. Find five of each of these.

Arctic skuas steal food from other birds. Spot two.

Puffins can use their wings like paddles to dive underwater for fish. Find three.

Killer whales catch seals by tipping up the ice so that they fall into the water. Spot three.

Little Auks gather in groups called rafts, while they look for food. Find ten.

Blue whales are probably the largest creatures that ever lived. Spot one.

Dolphin handle

Find a gold cup with dolphin handles.

Hand blower

Divers use hand blowers to blow away sand and uncover treasure. Spot two.

Barrel

Jar

Food for the ship's crew was stored in jars and barrels like these. Spot six of each.

Sometimes a diver makes a sketch of the ship. Spot a diver sketching.

Pirate treasure

Pirates were looking for chests full of coins. Spot seven.

In the 16th century, Spanish ships called galleons sailed from the Americas to Spain laden with gold, silver and jewels. Many were attacked by pirates. These divers are exploring a ship that sank with all her treasure.

Musket

Sword

Dagger

12

The ship's crew needed weapons to fight off the pirates. Find two of each of these.

Divers sometimes use metal detectors to help find buried treasure. Can you see one?

Find two gold plates.

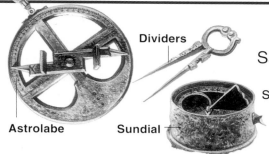
Astrolabe
Dividers
Sundial

Sailors navigated by the sun and stars. Find these measuring instruments.

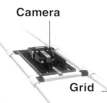
Camera
Grid

When divers find a wreck, they measure and photograph it. Can you see a camera?

Heavy things are attached to lifting bags which float to the surface. Find eight.

Silver ingot
Gold ingot

Gold and silver from South America were made into ingots in Mexico. Find seven silver and six gold ingots.

Small objects are brought to the surface in baskets. Can you spot six?

Find some divers measuring part of the wreck.

Cannon

Cannon-balls

The captain used this whistle to give orders to his crew. Can you find it?

Rich people sailed as passengers. Find these six jewels.

Gold locket
Rosary
Jewel encrusted buckle
Emerald ring
Emerald cross
Gold chain

Galleons built for battle had lots of cannons. Find 10 cannons and 20 cannonballs.

Spinner dolphins spin around in the air as they leap from the water. Spot ten.

Frigate birds steal food from other birds. Can you find two?

Divers study dangerous sharks from cages. Spot a diver in a cage.

Flying fish build up speed in the water and leap out to escape enemies. Spot seven.

A purse seine is a large circular net used to trap big shoals of fish. Can you see two?

The big blue sea

Manta rays are huge but harmless. They feed on tiny animals called plankton. Spot six.

Great white sharks, flying fish and many other huge, fast or dangerous creatures live right in the middle of the ocean. They swim close to the surface where there is more sunlight and plenty of food to eat.

Black and yellow sea snakes swim in groups. Spot 18 others.

Remoras hitch a lift on large fish and feed on their leftovers. Spot six.

Blue-striped marlins turn black or blue just before they eat. Find three.

14

Boobies fly across the water and dive down when they see a fish to eat. Spot six.

Great white sharks eat almost anything they find, even people. Spot three more.

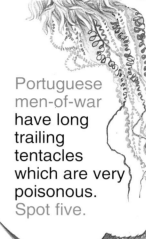

Portuguese men-of-war have long trailing tentacles which are very poisonous. Spot five.

Sailfish are the fastest fish in the sea. Can you find one?

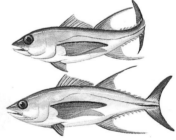

Yellow fin tuna often swim below dolphins. That's how fishermen sometimes find them. Spot six.

Dolphins can get caught in the nets by mistake. Spot five fishermen helping dolphins escape.

Leatherback turtles swim a long way to their breeding grounds. Spot four.

Whale sharks are the biggest sharks but they are not dangerous. Spot one.

15

The abyss

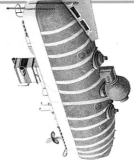

Tripod fish walk along the sea floor on long fins like legs. Find one.

Sonar "fish" are towed by ships. They record what's on the ocean floor. Spot three.

Bathyscaphes look like huge airships. They go into deep trenches. Can you see two?

Angler fish use a long fin with a light on the end to catch other fish. Can you see three?

Beardworms grow huge on food from the hot springs. Spot five groups.

The very deepest part of the ocean, called the abyss, is icy cold and dark. Explorers go down in small submarines, called submersibles. They have found volcanoes, hot springs, deep trenches, and some very strange creatures.

Nautile

Turtle

Alvin

Submersibles need thick walls, to stop the water above from crushing them. Spot each of these.

Deep sea spiders can be 50cm (20in) across. Can you see five?

Hatchet fish have two huge eyes on top of their heads. Spot 17.

16

Giant squid have huge eyes that are about 17 times the size of yours. Spot four.

Anemone

Vent fish

Crab

These strange creatures live and feed around the smokers. Find 20 of each.

Deep Flight is a submersible for the future. It will fly to the bottom fast. Can you see it?

Viper fish unhinge their jaws to gulp down large fish whole. Spot two.

Lantern fish have lights all along their bodies. Find 22.

Submersibles and ROVs have manipulator arms for picking things up. Spot five more.

Gulper eels swallow large fish with their wide mouths. Spot four.

Sperm whales dive deep for food, but they must swim to the surface to breathe. Can you find two?

ROVs are controlled by a cable from submersibles or ships. Can you see three?

Tall chimneys called black smokers grow up around hot springs. Find 15.

Coral dives

Millions of people dive for fun, and Australia's Great Barrier Reef is one of the best places to explore. The reef is made from the skeletons of billions of tiny creatures called corals. Can you find 15 divers here?

Sea slugs are small but they have bright markings. Spot each of these.

Underwater cameras need strong flash lights. Can you see four?

Flash light

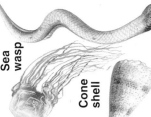

Sea wasp

Cone shell

Olive sea snake

These creatures are so poisonous, they can kill a person. Find one of each.

Fins help divers swim smoothly. Spot three yellow pairs.

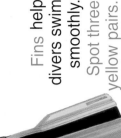

Giant clams grow very slowly and can live for a hundred years. Find two.

Tank

Regulator

Divers breathe compressed air from tanks. Spot a diver with two tanks.

Can you find three blue snorkels?

Snorkel

Mask

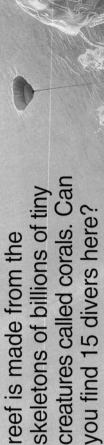

Can you find a leaking mask, half full of water?

"I'm OK"

"Let's go up"

Divers use hand signals to "talk" to each other. Spot two divers making each of these signals.

Sea fan

Staghorn coral

Brain coral

Corals are animals though some look more like rocks. Spot four clumps of each type.

Divers wear weights on their belts to help them descend. Find a diver with six weights.

Clown fish hide in poisonous anemones. Find nine others.

Barracudas are curious and sometimes follow a diver. Spot five.

Divers add air to jackets called BCs to go up, and let it out to go down. Spot a pink BC.

Hundreds of small fish live in the reef. Find three of each of these.

Surgeon fish

Clown Triggerfish

Moorish idol

Can you find four divers with knives?

Wetsuit

Knife

Can you see a diver in a short pink wetsuit like this one?

Air

Depth gauge

Consoles with dials show how much air is left and how deep it is. Find four.

Marker buoys on the surface show where the divers are. Can you see one?

As kelp crabs get bigger, they shed their shell and grow a new one. Spot six.

Sea stars stand on tiptoe to shed their eggs. Can you find two?

Bat rays glide through the forest on wing-like fins. Can you see three?

Ocean goldfish guard their space in the kelp fiercely. Find 11.

Sea otters wrap up in kelp when they snooze on the surface. Find eight.

Kelp forest

Giant kelp is the fastest growing plant in the world. It can grow 60cm (24in) in a day. Huge underwater kelp forests are home to thousands of creatures. People use the kelp too, to make things such as ice cream or paint.

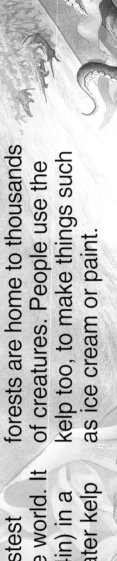

Gray whales shelter in the kelp to keep their babies safe. Spot a mother and her baby.

Sea snails eat their way up kelp plants. Spot 17.

Californian sealions are speedy swimmers and like to play. Spot three.

20

Blacksmith

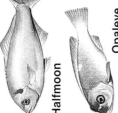

Halfmoon

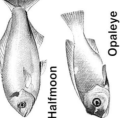

Opaleye

These fish live in large groups. They feed on the kelp. Spot 15 of each.

Giant kelpfish look like pieces of kelp, so they are hard to see. Can you find six?

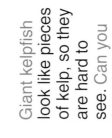

Giant octopuses grip their prey tightly with their strong tentacles. Find four.

Ships like this one harvest the kelp. Can you see the bottom of one?

Senoritas clean other fish and the kelp. Can you see five?

Abalones have beautiful shells. Spot one abalone and two empty shells.

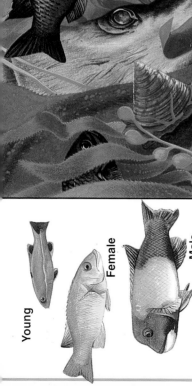

Young

Female

Male

Male, female and young sheephead wrasses all look different. Spot three of each.

Hungry sea urchins destroy the kelp. Find six red and six purple ones. Can you see three others?

Each kelp plant has a holdfast which clings to the rock. Can you see three others?

Oil rigs

Helmets let divers see and breathe easily. Find one with a square face plate.

Face plate

Rigs are built on land and then towed out to sea. Can you find five of them?

Newtsuit

Hard suits stop the water pushing in on the diver. The Newtsuit has legs with special joints. Find two.

Wasp

Wasp suits have propellers to help them move around in the water. Find five.

Conger eels have sharp teeth. They live in holes, so divers have to watch where they put their hands. Spot four.

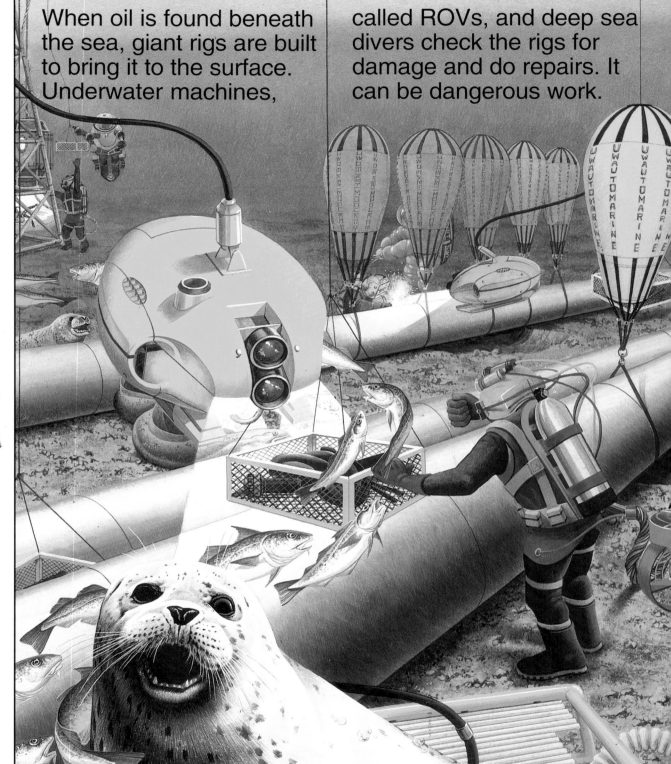

When oil is found beneath the sea, giant rigs are built to bring it to the surface. Underwater machines, called ROVs, and deep sea divers check the rigs for damage and do repairs. It can be dangerous work.

Diving bells are used to lower divers into deep water. Can you find three?

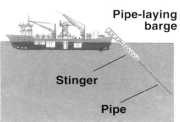
Pipe-laying barge

Stinger

Pipe

Pipes are laid by these special barges. Find one pipe-laying barge.

Special rods are heated up to cut metal. Spot three divers cutting.

Some seals are fierce and try to chase divers away. Spot five.

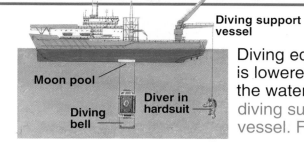

Diving support vessel

Moon pool

Diving bell

Diver in hardsuit

Diving equipment is lowered into the water from a diving support vessel. Find one.

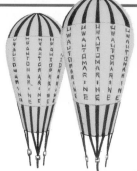

Airbags are used to support heavy things in the water. Spot ten.

Tools are lowered down from the surface in these baskets. Can you find five?

Work ROV

Different types of ROVs, (remotely operated vehicles) are used for each job. Work ROVs have mechanical arms. Spot three.

Eyeball ROV

Eyeball ROVs have cameras which video any damage and repairs. Spot six.

Gas

Hot water

Telephone line

Umbilicals join divers to a bell, bringing them gas and hot water. Spot six.

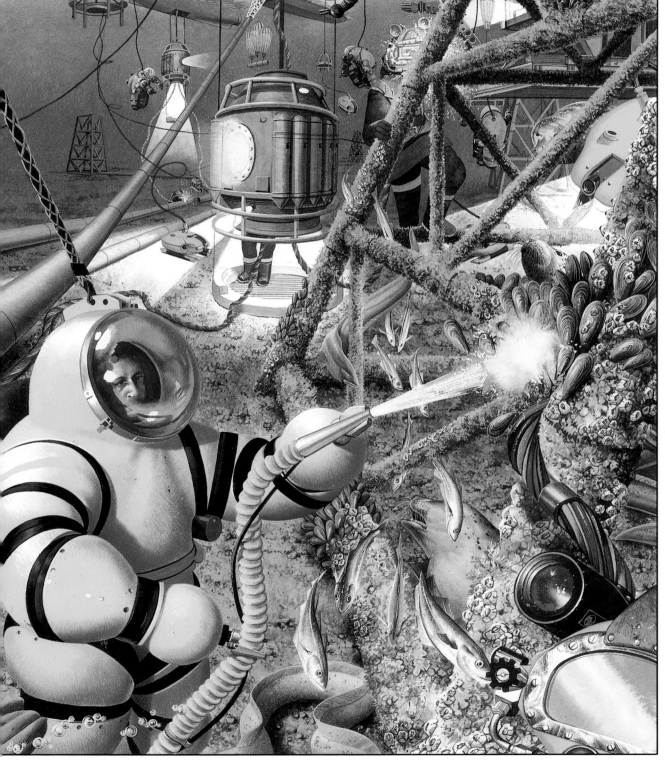

Mussels grow all over the rig and sometimes have to be cleaned off. Spot five groups.

Find 12 of each of these fish.

Pollack

Cod

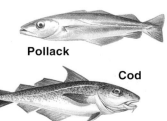

Water jet pumps are used for tasks such as cleaning. Can you see one?

The glossy ibis uses its long beak to catch shellfish, insects and even snakes. Spot four.

Otters paddle on the surface and dive down for food. Find three.

Soldier crabs can recognize each other by their bright blue shells. Spot 22.

Saltwater crocodiles are very dangerous and very large. Find three more.

Seaside jungle

Ospreys catch fish with their large feet and claws. Spot one.

The tangled roots of mangrove trees make a perfect home for many creatures. These trees grow in hot parts of the world where a river meets the sea. Their roots reach down into the water to help prop them up.

Dog-headed sea snakes slither through the water hunting for fish and crabs. Spot seven.

Mudskippers can use their fins like arms to drag themselves along the mud. Spot 25.

The mangrove roots are a good place for shellfish to breed. Spot 21 of each of these.

Oyster

Chama

Young tripletail fish hide on their sides near the surface. They look like dead leaves. Spot 12.

Ocean creatures often visit the mangroves to feed on plants. Can you spot two turtles?

Crab-eating macaques use their strong teeth to open shellfish. Spot two more.

When kingfishers spot a fish, they plunge head first after it. Can you see five?

Proboscis monkeys enjoy a swim. They often dive into the water to cool off. Spot five.

Some mangrove seedlings float for a year before planting themselves in the mud. Find 14.

Unlike most frogs, crab-eating frogs are quite happy in salt water. Spot three.

Male fiddler crabs use their enormous claw to fight off rivals. Spot three.

Swallow-tailed gull. Spot four.

Galápagos, Pacific Ocean

Volcanic islands

A few of these volcanic islands are still erupting. Can you find one?

Sealions surf in the waves for fun, but they must watch out for sharks. Find five.

Flightless cormorants hold their little wings out to dry after a dive. Spot one.

Common dolphin

Spotted dolphin

Dolphins come to the surface frequently for air. Find two of each of these types.

The Galápagos islands were formed by volcanoes erupting at the bottom of the sea. They are a very long way from any other land. Some of the creatures that live here are found nowhere else in the world.

Pelicans scoop up fish in the pouch under their beaks. Spot two.

Squid have two long arms and eight short ones. Find three.

A male frigate bird blows up his throat pouch to attract a mate. Spot two.

Pilot whales nudge their babies to the surface to breathe. Spot a mother and baby.

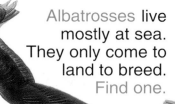

Albatrosses live mostly at sea. They only come to land to breed. Find one.

Fur seals get too hot in the midday sun, so they lie in the water to cool off. Spot two.

Red-footed booby

Blue-footed booby

Boobies make spectacular dives from 25m (82ft) high. Find four of each kind.

Sally lightfoot crabs have red shells and blue bellies. Can you see 25?

These penguins use their stubby wings to "fly" through the water. Spot eight.

Tiger sharks hunt alone. They swim all day, only stopping to eat. Can you find one?

Marine iguanas are lizards that can swim. They have to lie in the sun to warm up. Find 14 more.

Prehistoric seas 4-5

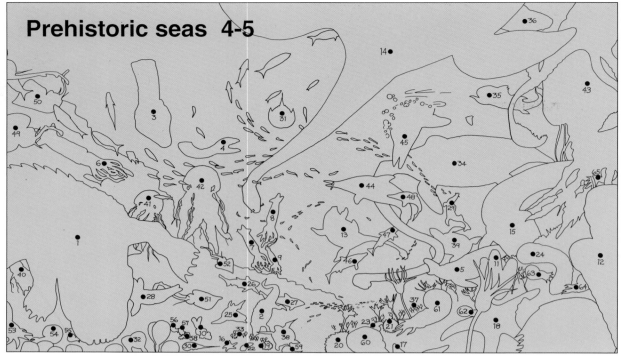

Shipwreck 6-7

Rocky shore 8-9

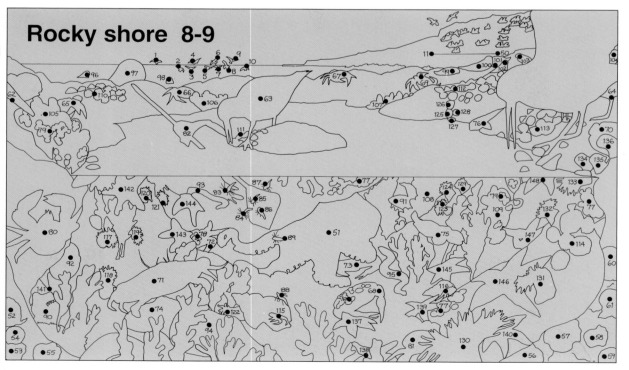

Icy seas 10-11

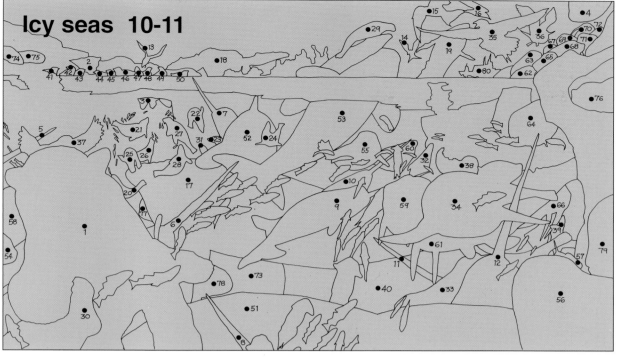

Polar bears 1 2 3 4
Narwhals 5 6 7 8 9 10 11 12
Arctic terns 13 14 15 16
Humpback whales 17 18
Harp seals 19 20 21 22 23 24
Ringed seals 25 26 27 28 29
Ribbon seals 30 31 32 33 34
Arctic skuas 35 36
Puffins 37 38 39
Blue whale 40
Little auks 41 42 43 44 45 46 47 48 49 50
Killer whales 51 52 53
Bearded seals 54 55 56
Transmitter 57
Walruses 58 59 60 61 62 63 64 65 66 67 68 69 70 71 72
Nautilus 73
Baby seals 74 75 76
Beluga whales 77 78 79
Research ship 80

Pirate treasure 12-13

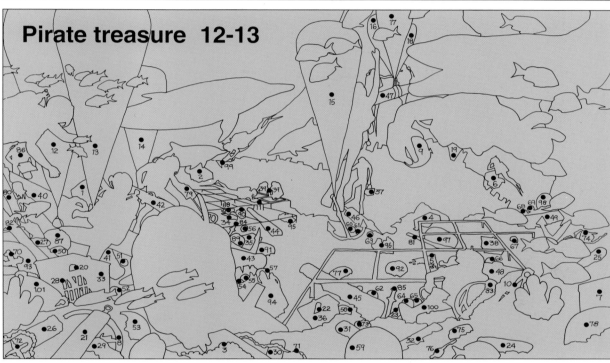

Chests of coins 1 2 3 4 5 6 7
Astrolabe 8
Sundial 9
Dividers 10
Camera 11
Lifting bags 12 13 14 15 16 17 18 19
Gold ingots 20 21 22 23 24 25
Silver ingots 26 27 28 29 30 31 32
Baskets 33 34 35 36 37 38
Divers measuring 39
Cannons 40 41 42 43 44 45 46 47 48 49
Cannonballs 50 51 52 53 54 55 56 57 58 59 60 61 62 63 64 65 66 67 68 69
Emerald cross 70
Gold chain 71
Rosary 72
Emerald ring 73
Gold locket 74
Buckle 75
Whistle 76
Gold plates 77 78
Metal detector 79
Muskets 80 81
Swords 82 83
Daggers 84 85
Diver sketching 86
Jars 87 88 89 90 91 92
Barrels 93 94 95 96 97 98
Hand blowers 99 100
Gold cup 101

The big blue sea 14-15

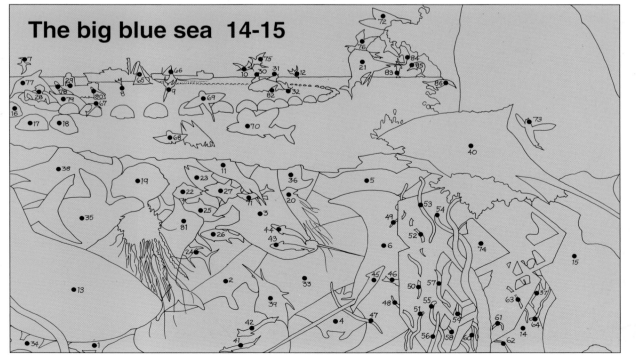

Manta rays 1 2 3 4 5 6
Boobies 7 8 9 10 11 12
Great white sharks 13 14 15
Portuguese men-of-war 16 17 18 19 20
Sailfish 21
Yellow fin tuna 22 23 24 25 26 27
Fishermen 28 29 30 31 32
Whale shark 33
Leatherback turtles 34 35 36 37
Marlins 38 39 40
Remoras 41 42 43 44 45 46
Sea snakes 47 48 49 50 51 52 53 54 55 56 57 58 59 60 61 62 63 64
Purse seine nets 65 66
Flying fish 67 68 69 70 71 72 73
Diver in cage 74
Frigate birds 75 76
Spinner dolphins 77 78 79 80 81 82 83 84 85 86

29

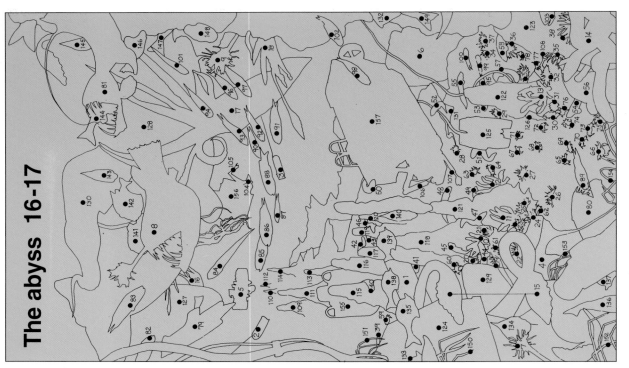

The abyss 16-17

Sonar "fish" 1 2 3
Tripod fish 4
Bathyscaphes 5 6
Angler fish 7 8 9
Beardworms 10 11 12 13 14
Giant squid 15 16 17 18
Anemones 19 20 21 22 23 24 25 26 27 28 29 30 31 32 33 34 35 36 37 38
Vent fish 39 40 41 42 43 44 45 46 47 48 49 50 51 52 53 54 55 56 57 58
Crabs 59 60 61 62 63 64 65 66 67 68 69 70 71 72 73 74 75 76 77 78
Deep Flight 79
Viper fish 80 81
Lantern fish 82 83 84 85 86 87 88 89 90 91 92 93 94 95 96 97 98 99 100 101 102 103

Manipulator arms 104 105 106 107 108
Black smokers 109 110 111 112 113 114 115 116 117 118 119 120 121 122 123
ROVs 124 125 126
Sperm whales 127 128
Gulper eels 129 130 131 132
Hatchet fish 133 134 135 136 137 138 139 140 141 142 143 144 145 146 147 148 149
Deep sea spiders 150 151 152 153 154
Submersibles:
    Turtle 155
    Alvin 156
    Nautile 157

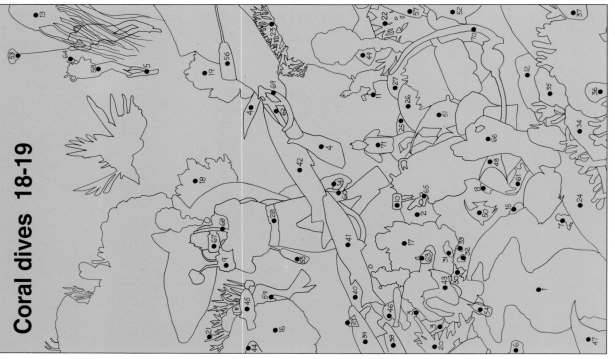

Coral dives 18-19

Giant clams 1 2
Yellow fins 3 4 5
Sea slugs 6 7 8
Cameras 9 10 11 12
Sea wasp 13
Olive sea snake 14
Cone shell 15
Coral:
    Sea fan 16 17 18 19
    Staghorn 20 21 22 23
    Brain 24 25 26 27
Diver with six weights 28
Clown fish 29 30 31 32 33 34 35 36 37
Barracudas 38 39 40 41 42
Pink BC 43
Clown triggerfish 44 45 46
Surgeon fish 47 48 49
Moorish idol 50 51 52
Marker buoy 53
Consoles 54 55 56 57

Diver in short pink wetsuit 58
Knives 59 60 61 62
Divers' signals:
    "Let's go up" 63 64
    "I'm OK" 65 66
Leaking mask 67
Blue snorkels 68 69 70
Diver with two tanks 71

Kelp forest 20-21

Sea otters 1 2 3 4 5 6 7 8
Ocean goldfish 9 10 11 12 13 14 15 16 17 18 19
Kelp crabs 20 21 22 23 24 25
Sea stars 26 27
Bat rays 28 29 30
Blacksmiths 31 32 33 34 35 36 37 38 39 40 41 42 43 44 45
Halfmoons 46 47 48 49 50 51 52 53 54 55 56 57 58 59 60
Opaleyes 61 62 63 64 65 66 67 68 69 70 71 72 73 74 75
Giant kelpfish 76 77 78 79 80 81
Giant octopuses 82 83 84 85
Ship 86
Senoritas 87 88 89 90 91
Abalone 92
Empty abalone shells 93 94
Holdfasts 95 96 97

Red sea urchins 98 99 100 101 102 103
Purple sea urchins 104 105 106 107 108 109
Sheephead wrasses:
    male 110 111 112
    female 113 114 115
    young 116 117 118
Sealions 119 120 121
Sea snails 122 123 124 125 126 127 128 129 130 131 132 133 134 135 136 137 138
Gray whales:
    mother 139
    baby 140

Oil rigs 22-23

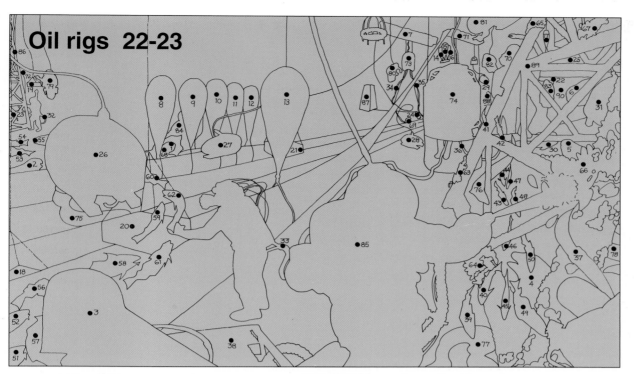

Helmet with square face plate 1
Seals 2 3 4 5 6
Diving support vessel 7
Airbags 8 9 10 11 12 13 14 15 16 17
Tool baskets 18 19 20 21 22
Work ROVs 23 24 25
Eyeball ROVs 26 27 28 29 30 31
Umbilicals 32 33 34 35 36 37
Water jet pump 38
Pollack 39 40 41 42 43 44 45 46 47 48 49 50
Cod 51 52 53 54 55 56 57 58 59 60 61 62
Mussels 63 64 65 66 67
Divers cutting 68 69 70
Pipe-laying barge 71
Diving bells 72 73 74
Conger eels 75 76 77 78

Wasp suits 79 80 81 82 83
Newtsuits 84 85
Rigs 86 87 88 89 90

Seaside jungle 24-25

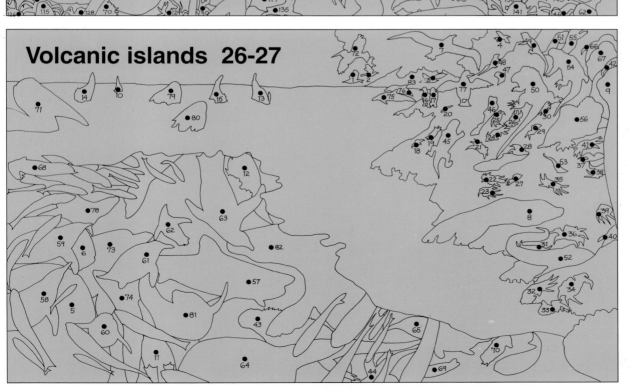

Osprey 1
Tripletail fish 2 3 4 5 6 7 8 9 10 11 12 13
Turtles 14 15
Crab-eating macaques 16 17
Kingfishers 18 19 20 21 22
Proboscis monkeys 23 24 25 26 27
Male fiddler crabs 28 29 30
Crab-eating frogs 31 32 33
Mangrove seedlings 34 35 36 37 38 39 40 41 42 43 44 45 46 47
Oysters 48 49 50 51 52 53 54 55 56 57 58 59 60 61 62 63 64 65 66 67 68
Chama 69 70 71 72 73 74 75 76 77 78 79 80 81 82 83 84 85 86 87 88 89
Mudskippers 90 91 92 93 94 95 96 97 98 99 100

101 102 103 104 105 106 107 108 109 110 111 112 113 114
Dog-headed sea snakes 115 116 117 118 119 120 121
Saltwater crocodiles 122 123 124
Soldier crabs 125 126 127 128 129 130 131 132 133 134 135 136 137 138 139 140 141 142 143 144 145 146
Otters 147 148 149
Glossy ibis 150 151 152 153

Volcanic islands 26-27

Swallow-tailed gulls 1 2 3 4
Pilot whale:
  adult 5
  baby 6
Albatross 7
Fur seals 8 9
Red-footed boobies 10 11 12 13
Blue-footed boobies 14 15 16 17
Sally lightfoot crabs 18 19 20 21 22 23 24 25 26 27 28 28 30 31 32 33 34 35 36 37 38 39 40 41 42
Marine iguanas 43 44 45 46 47 48 49 50 51 52 53 54 55 56
Tiger shark 57
Penguins 58 59 60 61 62 63 64 65
Male frigate birds 66 67
Squid 68 69 70
Pelicans 71 72
Spotted dolphins 73 74

Common dolphins 75 76
Cormorant 77
Sealions 78 79 80 81 82
Volcanic island erupting 83

Index